Corporate Credit Concepts

All rights reserved. No part of this book may be reproduced, stored in a retrieval system or transmitted in any form or by any means electronic, mechanical, photocopying, recording, or otherwise without express written permission of the author.

The material in the electronic publication can be stored only on one computer at one time and is intended for use by the purchaser. You may not forward, copy, or transfer this publication or part thereof, whether in electronic or in printed format, to another person or entity.

Every attempt has been made by the author to provide acknowledgement of the sources used for the material in this book.

Table of Contents

CORPORATE CREDIT CONCEPTS 1

Introduction 6
Separating Personal Credit from Business Credit 6
How to Establish a Business Credit Score....................................... 6
Establish Business Credit of Your Own... 7
Ensuring Your Business Credit File is Accurate................................ 8
Client Testimonials.. 9
How to get the most out of this book 13

CHAPTER 1 14

What is Business Credit?.. 14
How We Learned About Business Credit...................................... 17

CHAPTER 2 23

Why Build Business Credit? 23
The Business Credit Bureaus.. 28

CHAPTER 3 31

Requirements for Building Business Credit 31
Advantages of Forming an LLC 32
Advantages of an S Corporation 36
Advantages of a C Corporation 38
Shelf Corporations 44

CHAPTER 4 46

To be a Real Business You Must Look Like One........................... 46
Checking Your Personal Credit 49
Tax ID Number.. 49
411 Listing 50
Business License.. 51
Foreign filing... 51
Business Bank Account... 52
Business Bank Account Rating 53
Checklist 55

CHAPTER 5 57

Getting Set-Up with Dunn & Bradstreet 57
D&B Number 58
Option 1 58
Option 2 59
Option 3 60
eUpdate Password... 62
Understanding Your D&B Report 64
Financial Stress Score 73
Commercial Credit Score 74
Trade Credit 77
How are Corporate Experian and Equifax set up? 79

CHAPTER 6 81

What Do You Do After You Have Received Money from the Bank?
.... 81
Business Credit Cards 83

Personal Credit Inquiries 85
Business Lines of Credit 87
Equipment Leasing 88

CHAPTER 7 90

Maintaining Your D&B Report 90
Find Out Who is Reporting On Your Business.............................. 90

CHAPTER 8 93

Correcting Information on Your D&B Report................................ 93
About Your Company... 94
About Your Ownership... 96
About Management.. 98
About Your Operations 100

CHAPTER 9 104

How To Raise Your PAYDEX Score 104
PAYDEX Score.. 104
Percentage of Payments Within Terms 114
Maintaining Your Scores 116

CHAPTER 10 118

How to Remove Negative Items from Your Credit Report 118
How to Remove Collection Items from Your Report................... 118
How to Remove Financial Statements from Your Report............ 123
How to Remove Suits, Liens and Judgments............................... 125
UCC Filings 128

Bankruptcy 129

CHAPTER 11 132

Advanced Strategies for Building Business Credit 132

CD Deposit Program: Business Funding Without a Personal Guarantee 132

Increasing Credit Lines 134

DON'T MISS THE POINT OF BUILDING BUSINESS CREDIT 136

Bonus- 138

Introduction

In this book, you will learn some key things that will help you get you started building business credit. Here are just a few of the subjects that will be discussed.

Separating Personal Credit from Business Credit

You will learn how to keep your personal credit and business credit from combining and showing up together on your personal credit report. You will also learn how you can use your personal finances to finance your business or investments without the two types of credit being merged.

How to Establish a Business Credit Score

A lot of people will ask, "I have been around for a couple of years. Why does my business not have a credit score?" Usually, if you do not know that you have established business credit then you probably don't as it is not automatic when you start a business.

I will show you the step-by-step process of setting up your business credit report on your current business or on any business you plan on setting up in the future.

Establish Business Credit of Your Own

Many people do not realize that business credit even exists, nor do they know how to establish a business credit file. I will provide you with a step-by-step system that allows you to set up your business credit profile.

There are many do's and don'ts of setting up a business credit profile. It is essential that you have this information in order to do so properly and to be successful. It is very important that each step of this system is followed precisely. If a step is skipped or you don't complete one step before moving on, then you are going to hinder the ability of your business to operate at maximum capacity and to borrow money without having your personal credit report attached.

Ensuring Your Business Credit File is Accurate

This is extremely important, as the Fair Credit Reporting Act does not apply to businesses. If there is something wrong on your business credit report, or if you skip a step in setting it up, you have no legal recourse to have that information removed. If your file was set-up incorrectly, there is a good chance that your business credit file could be put in the "High Risk" category, making it near impossible to remove inaccuracies. Make sure to follow each step and take no short cuts. This is a proven step-by-step guide to properly establishing business credit.

Client Testimonials

"Unlimited Financing without a Personal Guarantee is the "financing bible" for our time! This book is packed full of financing resources and strategies that will teach you step by step how to get unlimited financing for your business. Read this book, apply what you learn and watch your business explode!"
Charrissa Cawley
Founder, www.reiconferences.com

"Cash is the life-blood of every business; it fuels your business growth. Most business failures are caused not by a shortage of good ideas or know how but by a lack of operating capital. Trent Lee has cracked the code on this vital area of your business. He makes available a much needed resource that you can use to fund your business, finance your investments and achieve your business goals and dreams. I highly recommend that you make him a member of your wealth team."
Drew Miles, The Wealth Building Attorney

If you are in business then you MUST learn how to separate your business credit from your Personal credit. Trent Lee's new book teaches the foundation and advanced techniques that 99% of business owners don't know- FIRED UP!

John Di Lemme, Millionaire Maker

If you want to get corporate credit so you can grow your business, fund a project or just need more funds then Trent Lee's new book is the one thing you need to read right now.

Matt Bacak, Frontier Marketing Intl, LLC.

"Before I start any new venture, I always contact Trent and Chad Lee first. Working with them, we have credit lines in place well before we need the money. In the jungle of business credit offers, changing requirements and piles of paperwork, it makes sense to have an expert working for you. The Lee's are experts you can trust. Follow them and their concepts and you will get the credit you need."

Warren Whitlock, BestSellerAuthors.com

"Corporate Credit Concepts has built a foolproof system. My business credit coach walked me through step by step until I had the amount of cash credit I was in need of...$175,000!"

Jose Acuna
Acuna Electric

"Corporate Credit Concepts made the process of separating my personal credit from my business credit so easy. Thanks a lot. You made it possible to take my business to the next level."

Jacob Dunn

"I never thought of purchasing a shelf corporation. My business credit coach helped me obtain over $200,000!'"

Mathew Ethan
Accurate Financial, Inc

"I now have the ability to take my company to the next level. Thanks to you guys I was able to secure over $200,000 in unsecured business lines of credit."

Maria Santana

"Unfortunately, I went through another business credit building company that charged over $1000 upfront with no guarantee. The only thing I ended up with is a business credit file and some vendor credit...no cash

www.corporatecreditconcepts.com

credit! Once I started working with Corporate Credit Concepts I was able to obtain over $100,000 in CASH credit. Thanks guys!"

Andrew Jensen
Crotochrom, Inc

www.corporatecreditconcepts.com

How to get the most out of this book

I would recommend reading the book in its entirety first. This way you get a better feel for the credit building process and can start to see the end from the beginning. After you have read it once I would recommend following the step by step checklist as you build business credit on your own. We have outlined all the necessary steps that need to be completed in order to successfully build your business credit.

Because of the many situation and conditions that can arise during your credit building process that cannot possibly all be covered in a book I have included our phone number and email address. Please feel free to call or email if we can help you in any way.

Happy Borrowing!

Trent Lee and Chad Lee
702-216-0450
Trentlee@corporatecreditconcepts.com

Chapter 1

What is Business Credit?

If you have ever strolled through the business section of your local bookstore, then you know that there are many books on running a business. Topics range from how to start your business, grow your business and even how to become a millionaire by purchasing and selling real estate. As an avid reader, I have read numerous books and found many of them have provided some sort of information that was useful. However, there is a lack of information on how to finance your business, especially when it comes to building business credit that will allow you to finance, operate and expand.

This is why I have written this book. I have talked with thousands of people who are business owners, real estate investors, and entrepreneurs and none of them have had any idea of what business credit is!

If you have a business, or if you are starting a business, then this book will help you in the area of financing your business. If you are interested in becoming a real estate investor, then this book will help you in your investments. You will find that business credit will be vital to the success of your business.

The more money you have to start and grow the business, the more likely your business will succeed. According to the Census Bureau's 2002 survey of businesses, one third of the general business population has less than $5,000 for start up capital, while half of the companies on the Inc. 500 list were started with at least $50,000. In fact, banks, which say they want to help small business owners, turn down over 97% of their business loan applications. This means that in order to receive credit for your business, you have to use your personal assets, such as your home, to secure your business loans. This defeats the purpose of setting up a corporation or limited liability company in which your personal assets are to be protected if you are required to use them as collateral for business financing.

How can any small business receive funding when they are required to produce documentation such as the following?

- Interim financial statements
- Most recent Federal Tax Returns for each principal owner
- Accountant prepared financial statements including Profit & Loss statement and Balance Sheet for the last 3 years
- Personal financial statements for each principal owner
- Organization papers, such as incorporation papers, DBA papers, business licenses, etc.
- List of business and personal assets that can be used as collateral
- Names and contact information for at least three credit references

These documents can be very difficult for a start-up

business to supply to a bank, especially if they have never done any business before. Many banks expect a business to be already established before they request financing, but you can get started without it!

Let me stress this. Keeping your personal credit separate from your business credit is a must. This does not mean that you cannot provide a personal guarantee, but you do not want your personal debt and your business debt to be combined. This will ensure that your personal credit scores are not affected by your business credit.

How We Learned About Business Credit

As real estate investors, my father and I want to ensure that we maintain good personal credit scores. As we reviewed our personal credit reports, we realized that there were several credit cards missing. This was alarming at first, until we realized that the missing credit cards were our business credit cards. Even though we had supplied our social security number and guaranteed these cards personally, they had not been reported on our personal credit report! As we applied for additional business credit cards for more funding, we realized that they did not show up on our credit report either. It was like invisible debt! No one would even realize the available credit we had by looking at our personal credit reports.

As we started to experiment with more business credit cards, we found the same occurrence. These cards were not reported back to the credit bureaus under our personal credit report. We also noticed that the interest rates were lower than what we received on personal credit cards. As an added bonus, we discovered that all of the interest we paid on our business lines of credit and credit cards were tax deductions, where that interest would not have been if on personal credit cards.

At this point we had found another property to invest in. The property had a lot of equity and we had to move quickly. We went to the bank and they turned us down! We couldn't believe it. Many of the banks told us the same thing; our debt to income ratio was too high. We had been using corporations to show as little personal income as possible and had 13 mortgages in our name. Even though the properties were rentals and bringing in cash, they still turned us down.

We then realized we had to learn how to separate our personal credit from our business credit. We began searching for someone who could teach us how to develop good business credit. Unfortunately, we could not find anyone who was honest and reputable, so we had to learn the hard way. We had to learn it ourselves.

As the years went by we became more experienced at developing business credit to use for our own businesses and investments. At this time, a national company offered to purchase our family business. My father had started the business in his early 20's, more than 25 years prior. It was the largest company in Nevada for its industry and had grown to over 500 employees.

We weren't interested in selling, but we were curious about what they would offer us. The national company sent auditors in for two weeks and then made an astounding offer. We had no idea that they would offer so much. We decided to sell the company to them and follow the trend of making money on the stock market. We were making such astounding returns we soon decided to put *all* of the money in the stock market.

The year was 1999 and as you might imagine, most of the money was in tech and dot com stocks. We quickly went from multiple seven-digit figures in our stock portfolio to less than $15,000!

With such a crushing loss, we realized it was time to sell off our toys. We sold our cars, boats, houseboats, and cabins and liquidated some of our residential properties. We then invested $200,000 into a new business that we were just starting with a partner. My father and I had dedicated our time and efforts fully to this business and then the partner disappeared to California with all of our money!

We were left with only a few commercial buildings to offset our monthly expenses. We had completely relied on this new business and now it was gone. We did have one thing and that was our knowledge of business credit, so we began to rebuild our business credit, mostly to finance our living expenses and to support our families and partly to fund another new business.

Things didn't take off as quickly as we had hoped and I began looking for a job. I needed something to help support my family so that I could help with the business during the day. The only thing I could find on quick notice was a janitor position at night.

Those days were humbling for me. I realized how hard it is to get a business going and then take it to the next level. The main reason it was so difficult was because we had no financing. We were building our business credit to pay for our personal bills, but we couldn't build it fast enough to finance the business. If it had not been for the business credit, we would have had to declare bankruptcy.

There are a couple of lessons that I will never forget from those days.

1. Always have more credit than you need
2. Pay interest only on what you use

If you have a lot of credit that you don't use, that's okay. You don't have to pay anything for it. I can personally relate to the national statistic that 50% of small businesses fail in the first year and 95% fail within the first five years. The number one reason for this is lack of financing. If we had not built our business credit, we would have never been one of the top companies in the nation for building business credit and for aiding business owners in separating their personal credit from their business credit.

Chapter 2

Why Build Business Credit?

If you have been in business for years, you may not know what business credit is. You may also be wondering why you should begin building it now.

For years, good companies have been declined by banks because of incorrect information on their business credit report. In most cases, companies are being declined because they do not have a business credit report at all. The truth is that lenders and creditors have few options in getting the credit information they need. D&B is one of the only companies who publish the information that it receives. Unlike personal credit, where the three major bureaus collect and report information, there is only one major company that collects business information and publishes it. This company is Dun & Bradstreet. There are others that may also collect business information, but they are nowhere near as large as D&B. Most lending institutions incorporate the information and use the commercial scoring model that is retrieved from D&B's database.

When you apply for credit for a business, most creditors will pull your business credit report. This credit can be for anything for your business from credit cards, loans or equipment. What happens if they pull your business credit report and there is nothing there? They will rely on your personal credit to guarantee your request. When they see there is no business credit file, they are not able to lend as much credit to the business. One of the main reasons that you need a business credit report is for the ability to receive more funding.

However, there are several other important reasons as well. The main reason is that by building business credit you are able to keep it separate from your personal credit. Over 65% of businesses will start-up through their personal credit cards. Over 50% of existing business will continue to use personal credit cards to pay for business expenses. They are just hoping that one day they will be able to pay themselves back.

If you begin with business credit, then you can keep your business credit and personal credit separate from day one. I cannot count the times I have seen a business owner begin a business on personal credit cards and then not be able to pay themselves back as quickly as they want. They are in need of additional money and the only money they can get is through their personal credit cards. Their personal credit cards are then maxed out and their debts to income ratios steadily rise. When this occurs, their personal credit scores begin to steadily drop. No lender will lend money to a business with an owner in this type of situation.

If you begin your business with business credit, then your business debt will not affect you personally. Because of this, your personal credit scores will remain high because your business debts are not being reported on your personal credit file. This means that when you need to go obtain additional financing, your scores will be high.

Another reason that you should set-up business credit is so that you don't have to guarantee the financing with your personal assets. This will not occur instantly, but our goal is to stop giving your personal guarantee for your business. If you build your business credit properly then it will stand on its own when you need financing. In order for you to successfully do this, you need to follow the process of building business credit.

There is still one more reason that you need to build business credit – to save money! This is the most important reason. By building business credit you *can* save yourself and your business money. How does this work? Here's an example:

Let's suppose that you need $50,000 for a piece of equipment for your business. Without D&B, your bank will use your personal credit only. If you get approved, you will have in this example an interest rate of 18%. With a D&B report, you can lower your rate to 10% **and** you do not have to guarantee the loan with your personal assets.

Here's a quick comparison:

	Without D&B	With D&B
Lease Amount	$50,000	$50,000
Interest Rate	18%	10%
Term of Lease	60 months	60 months
Advance Payments	0	0
End of Lease Option	$1 Buy Out	$1 Buy Out
Monthly Payment	$1,269.67	$1,062.35
Total Payments	$76,180.20	$63,741.00
Total Savings		$12,439.20

By simply building business credit and setting up your business properly you can literally save yourself tens of thousands of dollars! When it comes to the bottom line, you have to be concerned as a business owner.

The final reason that you need to build business credit is that the business credit bureaus are in business for the same reason as the personal credit bureaus are – they sell your information. Why is this important to you? Because, for example, Citibank, American

Express or other credit companies may go to D&B and ask for information on all of the businesses who have been incorporated for the last six months. These companies will then send out "pre-approval" applications to those businesses on the list that they bought. Most of us know this as junk mail – right? But, it may not be trash if you are a business owner. You can actually build business credit through that lender if they go to D&B and request the information for those businesses that have a PAYDEX score of 80+, financial stress class 1, credit score class 2 and a D&B rating of 1R3. These businesses are receiving an entirely different type of "pre-approval" from these companies. They are completely different than the ones you are receiving without business credit. Needless to say they are much better offers!

The Business Credit Bureaus

Let me give you a brief introduction to the different business credit bureaus.

Dun & Bradstreet was started back in the 1800's and has been collecting business information for over 150 years. They compile the information that they gather and then they sell it to other companies. The most important fact for you to know is that they are the largest and most predominant business bureau that is in the marketplace.

You should also be aware that other companies have entered the business credit world as well. Experian, who you know as a personal credit bureau, now has a business division called Corporate Experian. Several lenders now base their lending decisions on Corporate Experian instead of D&B. Equifax is also entering the business credit world and they are offering an extensive business credit report. There are a few others, but they are not big players and you won't need to worry too much about them. These include PayNet, FDInsight, BusinessCreditUSA, and ClientChecker.

We will go into more detail later on what a business credit report contains and how to read it.

You may be wondering if you even have a business

credit report. If you don't know, then more than likely you don't have one! Business credit is set up differently from personal credit. It is not like your personal credit in the sense that when you turned 18 and got your first credit card, you immediately had a credit report.

This is a very important fact that I cannot stress enough. You must follow the steps of setting up a proper business, before you establish your file. We will go into the details later, but there are prerequisites that you need to meet before you begin to set up a business credit file. You must know what to do, the order to do these steps in and then manually set up a D&B credit file to ensure that the information is completely accurate.

Chapter 3

Requirements for Building Business Credit

First, I need to make a clarification. Unless you are incorporated or a limited liability company, then you might be "in business," but you are not "a business." You must be a corporation or an LLC in order to build true business credit. If you are not, you will not be able to separate your person credit from your business credit.

If you do not have a business entity, then you may contact us at (702) 216-0450. We can set up a business entity for you. The entire process can be done for you quickly. In order to capitalize on business financing that is available and to separate business and personal credit, you have to have a real business entity.

Business credit cannot and does not exist for a sole

proprietor. All that a sole proprietor has available are personal loans or lines of credit. This credit is tied to your personal social security number.

What type of entity do you need? You will need to consult your CPA, tax attorney or lawyer for advice on what type of entity will fit your business best. You can be either a corporation or limited liability company to build business credit.

Advantages of Forming an LLC

An LLC is a hybrid between a partnership and a corporation. The LLC combines the "pass-through" treatment a partnership has with the limited liability of a corporation.

An LLC is unlike a corporation, which can have as few as one shareholder. Most states require that an LLC consist of two or more members. Some states, however, require an LLC to have two or more owners. There are some states that are allowing single member LLCs, but they are treated differently than an

LLC with multiple members.

Like limited partnerships and corporations, an LLC is recognized as a separate legal entity from its members.

One of the greatest benefits is that the LLC is only responsible for the company's debts. This shields the members from individual liability. There are some exceptions to this when it pertains to the individual members.

- **Guarantor Liability:** When an LLC member has personally guaranteed the obligations of an LLC, then he or she will be held liable. For example, if an LLC is a relatively new business or has no credit history then a prospective landlord may lease office space to the LLC, but will most likely require a personal guarantee from the members.
- **Alter Ego Liability:** This is similar to the judicial doctrine that is applied to corporations where the court may hold the individual

shareholders liable when they use the corporation as an "alter ego" to protect their own assets. An LLC can be held liable for debts if the courts choose to impose the "alter ego liability" doctrine. This is also known as "piercing the corporate veil." Please note, a corporation is responsible for meeting the necessary corporate formalities such as annual shareholder meetings and documenting important decisions with minutes, resolutions and written consents signed by the directors or shareholders.

Management and control of the LLC is vested to its members, unless the articles of organization are written otherwise. Voting interest in an LLC directly corresponds to interest in profits, unless the articles of the organization provide differently. No one can become a member of the LLC without the consent of members having a majority in interest, unless the articles of organization are written otherwise.

Many states will now allow an LLC to have a

perpetual existence. In the past, an LLC was required to specify a date that the LLC would terminate. Now, an LLC may dissolve at the death, withdrawal, resignation, expulsion or bankruptcy of a member. This is true unless a majority of both the profits and capital interests vote to continue the LLC within 90 days.

The existence of an LLC begins when the Articles of Organization are filed with the Secretary of State. These articles must be on the form provided by the Secretary of State and list the latest date at which the LLC will dissolve along with a statement noting if the LLC is managed by one manager, more than one manager or the members.

Members of an LLC must enter into an Operating Agreement to validate the formation of the LLC. This agreement may come into existence either before or after filing the Articles of Organization. This agreement may be either oral or in writing.

ntages of an S Corporation

An S corporation begins an existence as a for profit corporation upon filing the Article of Incorporation at the state level. To form the S corporation, you must file as a regular corporation and then convert to an S corporation by filing the IRS Form 2553. To start your business off as an S corporation, you must file this form within 75 days of the start of the tax year for your corporation.

The IRS has rules on who can establish an S corporation. These include:

- An S corporation cannot consist of more than 100 shareholders.
- None of an S corporation's shareholder can be non-resident aliens. This means a shareholder cannot be a non-citizen who does not live in the US.
- S corporations can only have one class of stock.
- S corporation shareholders can only be individuals, estates, or certain trusts.

Corporations cannot be shareholders of an S corporation.

Owners who want the best of both worlds of a corporation and a sole proprietor may choose an S corporation. They are taxed as a sole proprietor and at the same time they have the limited liability of a corporation. There are other benefits as well including savings on self-employment taxes.

The corporate income and losses are passed through to the shareholders. The shareholders must split stock ownership and report the income on their individual tax returns. An S corporation will normally pay no taxes but will file information with the IRS on Form 1120-S, which indicates how much the business has earned or lost and each shareholders portion of the corporate income or loss.

As an S corporation, you are unable to split your income between two separate taxpaying individuals. This is the main drawback to an S corporation; however a lot of start-up businesses do not make enough at first to warrant income splitting. If you grow large enough then this may be an option. An important tax benefit comes with your ability to save on your Social Security and Medicare taxes. All businesses are required to pay this tax, except corporations. This tax does not have to be paid on distributions from your S corporation. This means the more net profits you pass on through the corporation to yourself, the less in taxes you are required to pay.

Advantages of a C Corporation

The C corporation is the standard designation on a general-for-profit corporation. An incorporator must file Articles of Incorporation and pay the requisite state fees as well as prepaid taxes with the appropriate agency. This may be a Secretary of State or Corporations Division.

A corporation is an entity in itself. It assumes a separate legal and tax life that is distinct and separate from its shareholders. The corporation pays taxes on its own corporate income tax rates and files corporate tax forms each year. A corporation's management and control is in its board of directors who are elected by the shareholders of the corporation. Directors generally make policy and other major decisions regarding the corporation. They do not individually represent the corporation in dealing with third persons. Dealings with third persons are handled through the corporation's officers and employees.

The shareholders of a corporation are actually the owners of a corporation. The Board of Directors are responsible for the management and policy decisions of the corporation. There are a few instances when the shareholders are required to approve the Actions of the Board of Directors. For example, amendment to the articles of incorporation, sale of corporate assets, mergers, etc.

Corporate officers are elected by the Board of Directors and are responsible for day-to-day operational activities of the corporation. Corporate officers include the president, vice-president, secretary and treasurer. One person may actually fulfill all of the roles of the corporate officers. Some states, however, may require the number of persons required to manage a corporation be at least equal to the number of owners. If there are two shareholders, for example, there must be two minimum directors.

Corporations also have the ability to offer employees unique fringe benefits such as health insurance, disability, etc. Owner-employees may deduct health insurance premiums paid by the corporation from corporate income. Corporate defined benefit plans also offer better retirement options than those that are offered by non-corporate plans.

There are also several corporate formalities that pertain to corporations. They have the benefits of limited liability as well as special tax treatment, but those who run the corporation must observe corporate formalities. Even a one-person corporation must wear the various hats and are responsible for the various formalities associated with each position. If a thinly capitalized corporation is created, funds commingled, stock never issued and other formalities are never followed, then the IRS may "pierce the corporate veil" and hold the shareholders responsible personally for the business debt.

Corporations are taxed for their own profits and any profits that are paid out in the form of dividends are taxed again to the recipient. Small corporations, however, rarely pay dividends. Instead they are owner-employees and are paid salaries and fringe benefits that are deductible to the corporation. The result is that the employee-owners end up paying income taxes on the business income and double taxation rarely occurs in these small business settings.

Discuss the options of S and C corporations with your accountant or CPA and get advice on which form will be best for you. These professionals know the details of your business as far as finances and taxes go and should be able to provide you with this information.

As a separate legal entity, the corporation may continue indefinitely. The existence of a corporation is not affected by the death of the owner, not its shareholders, officer, directors or the transference of shares.

A corporation is not considered a "citizen" under the privileges of the Fourteenth Amendment of the U.S. constitution. A corporation may exercise some constitutional protections of a natural citizen such as:

- **Right to Due Process and Equal Protection:** Corporations enjoy the right to equal protection and due process under both the Fourteenth and Fifth Amendments. They are also protected under similar provisions in the California Constitution.
- **Freedom of Speech:** Corporations have the right to express themselves on matters of public important, even if the corporation is not affected "materially." This right is absent of some narrowly drawn restrictions under state interest.
- **Right to Counsel:** A corporation cannot be imprisoned, but criminal action may be in the form of fines or penalties that may harm

shareholders, officers and other persons. A corporate criminal defendant does have the protection of the Sixth Amendment in that they have the right to counsel. A corporation faces no risk of incarceration, and it has no right to appointed counsel if it cannot afford to retain private counsel.

- **No Privilege Against Self-Incrimination:** Corporations have no privilege against self-incrimination. For example, to prevent disclosure of incriminating corporate records.

Type of Company	Liability	Operations	Management	Raising Capital
Sole Proprietorship	Unlimited	Simple	Proprietor	Difficult
General Partnership	Partners	Simple	Partners	Difficult
Limited Liability Company	No	Medium	Members	Very Possible
Corporations	No	Difficult	Board	Definitely
Non-Profit Corporations	No	Difficult	Members or Trustees	Definitely
Professional Corporations	Varies by State	Difficult	Board/ Licensed Professionals	Definitely

Shelf Corporations

Many of you may have heard of "Shelf Corporations," if you have not then you may want to consider the benefits of purchasing a shelf corporation if you have not been in business for more than 2 years. Banks will typically choose to lend to businesses that have been in business for more than 24 months. The banks will verify the date of incorporation by searching for the business on the secretary of state website. This means that you cannot run out and incorporate on December 31st and have it count as a year in business on January 1st. Unfortunately, there are companies out there teaching this myth. It simply does not count; the banks will determine how long you have been in business by the month and date of incorporation, not the year.

I will not be going into great detail about shelf corporations. While it is possible to obtain financing for new businesses, it is much easier to obtain even more financing for businesses that have been around for more than 2 years. We have many shelf corporations as an option if you choose, please call us; you will not be able to find shelf corporations cheaper anywhere else. We will analyze your specific situation and help you determine if a shelf corporation is the best option for you.

Important: Please make sure to speak with us before purchasing a shelf corporation, we need to determine if your situation warrants the cost incurred to obtain one.

Chapter 4

To be a Real Business You Must Look Like One

Banks are not donation centers and they require you to meet precise specifications if they are going to even think about lending you money. In order to build excellent business credit and to obtain financing for your business, not only do you have to look like a real business, you have to be one! You can not use a post office box or virtual office; this looks very funny to a bank. In fact, you will get an automatic rejection from some lenders. Your business has to be located somewhere after all – right? A P.O. Box, virtual office or mail forwarding address is not the right place for your business.

You can use your home address for business credit building, but be aware that some lenders will not fund "home based" businesses either. There are several services that will set up your business with a physical address. You may also contact executive suite office buildings and lease an actual office space. Do make sure that the address is appropriate and you have a separate suite number only for your business. You will need to make sure that no other businesses share your suite number.

Remember, this must be a physical location that you can actually operate business from. These executives' suites will also professionally answer the phone on behalf of your business. They will then forward the call to the phone number that you provide them. You must also have a separate business phone number that is listed under the business name in the 411 information directory. Do not use your home phone or your cell phone. This needs to be a phone number that is professionally answered and equipped with voice mail in the name of your business.

There are many providers that will offer a service called "call forwarding." Any time someone calls, the call will automatically be forwarded to your cell phone or another number of your choice. They will also list the number in the 411 information directory for you. You do not want to use this type of service. The reason why is because many lenders will want you to call from your business phone to activate your credit card, when you call and your business name and phone shows on their caller id the system will automatically activate your account. If you have a "call forwarding" number, you may be able list it with 411 but you cannot make phone calls from that line.

Be certain that your business name is spelled correctly on the Secretary of State website, business credit bureaus, and other vendors that you will set up. You also need to make certain that the address is correct. If the address is not exact, your good payment history will not be reported properly. Remember that "Street" and "St." will make a big difference as will other characters such as a "#" before your suite number, etc.

Checking Your Personal Credit

It is recommended that you order a monthly credit monitoring service that will notify you of all changes on your personal credit report. You will also be able to dispute any inaccuracies as well. This is not required, but is good common sense to ensure your personal credit report is accurate.

You can build your business credit regardless of your personal credit, but it is much easier if you have a credit score of 680 or higher and no negative items on the report. If you have any negative items or too many inquiries please consider working with a reputable credit repair organization while building your business credit.

Tax ID Number

A Tax ID number (EIN Number) is very important. Without a Tax ID, your business will be useless. A Tax ID identifies your business and your information. It is similar to that of a Social Security number but identifies you as a business, not as a personal entity. If you need to acquire a Tax ID number, then you will need to fill out the IRS Form SS-4. These are very easy to obtain online at www.irs.gov.

411 Listing

Your business phone number, your business name and your business address should be listed together in a 411 information directory. This is very important! Do not use your home phone number or cell phone number as the number will be listed as a personal residence, not a business! The phone needs to be professionally answered and have a voice mail with the name of your business.

Many clients ask us if they can use a "call forwarding number" or a VOIP number. Do not use this type of phone number. Your phone number should be a landline business number and have a local area code, not an 800 number. Many lenders will want you to call an automated activation account from the business phone number. If your business phone number is not listed on the lender's caller ID, they will not be able to activate your account.

Business License

All businesses should have a business license. You should also check with your state, city or county to verify what type of license and permit you require. This is a very important step that cannot be emphasized enough. The business credit bureaus will verify whether you are operating with a license and then post those findings on your business credit report. If you do not have a license, you risk not being able to borrow money from a lender, as many lenders will pull the report and look for whether or not you are operating with a license.

There are times when your local or state authorities might not require you to obtain a business license. Even though you are not required, we still recommend that you apply for one. Having a business license will make it easier when Dunn and Bradstreet do their investigation and when you apply for lines of credit at the bank.

Foreign filing

If you live and operate your business in one state and

you have an out-of-state corporation, you will need to make sure that your corporation is filed as foreign in the state where you operate business.

Business Bank Account

Most businesses will already have a business account set up. If so, you will still want to pay close attention to this information. If not, you will need to set-up a business bank account and you will be required to supply the following:

- Articles of Incorporation
- List of officers or members/managers
- Copy of Operating Agreement
- EIN Number
- Two forms of identification
- Possibly additional information depending on the bank

Once you have your account set up, the name of the business checking account needs to be identical to the legal spelling of the business name. Be certain that the phone number and address are also correct.

Setting up the bank account correctly is a vital part of building business credit.

Business Bank Account Rating

Your business banking account reflects how you manage your business. It will show how successful you are, your ability to repay your debts, and how you handle your business debts and expenses. Accounts that carry a low balance can deter lenders when they are applying for financing. The average amount of the business account carries will generate a bank rating. Lenders often use your rating as an indicator for whether or not to lend money to your business.

There are two tiers to these ratings. The first is the balance rating. Your average minimum balance maintained in your account over a period of three months calculates this rating.

Bank Rating	Account Balance	Bank Rating	Account Balance
Low 4	$1,000 - $3,999	Low 5	$10,000 - $39,000
Mid 4	$4,000 - $6,999	Mid 5	$40,000 - $69,999
High 4	$7,000 - $9,999	High 5	$70,000 - $99,999

To obtain the best bank rating you will want to maintain a "low 5." Many lenders will often consider anything less than a "low 5" risky.

I recommend that you work your balance up to $10,000, even if you need to borrow form personal funds. You can simply allow it to sit in the account so that you are able to obtain a "low 5." If you are unable to attain this level, you will be okay. There are lenders who will still lend to your business. The end result is not the money we are helping you obtain, but the fact that you are setting up the business credit score properly. This will allow you to get the money you need to obtain and qualify for additional financing long after you are done dealing with us.

With good business credit scores you will also be able

to receive a large number of "pre-approval" offers that will allow you to qualify for additional financing. The money that we are able to help you obtain is just a start.

The second rating that you will obtain is based on how often you use the account. For example, bounced checks can destroy your business bank rating.

Checklist

Up to this point, you should have completed the following tasks for your business.

- ✓ Entity Formation
- ✓ Tax ID
- ✓ 411 Listing
- ✓ Business License
- ✓ Foreign filing (if needed)
- ✓ Business Bank Account
- ✓ Business Bank Account Rating

If you have not completed these steps, then *do not*

move forward.

Chapter 5

Getting Set-Up with Dunn & Bradstreet

At this point you should have completed all of the previous steps in Chapter 4. If so, you are ready to set up your D-U-N-S® Number. If you have been to the Dunn & Bradstreet website, you have found one of two things. First, you may not be able to find a report on your business at all. Secondly, if you have found a report then the report may have a DS rating. This means that D&B has not collected enough information on your business.

Typically, this is because nobody has accessed your D&B Business Credit Report and there has not been a corporate verification or investigation. This means that we have to start from scratch on building your credit score.

If you have found a copy of your report, then it may be full of errors that must be corrected. Since you will be building your business credit report from the bottom up, you will be able to correct this information. We will assume here that they have no information on you at all.

D&B Number

Option 1

A D-U-N-S® Number can be set up free through www.dnb.com. Under the Customer Resources heading, click on "Get a D&B D-U-N-S® Number. You will then be directed to begin the process by checking if your company is listed in the D&B database. You will also be asked to choose "Establish a credit file with ScoreBuilder and get a D-U-N-S® number" or "Get a D-U-N-S® number only". You will choose get a D-U-N-S® number only.

After you have set-up your D-U-N-S® number for your business, it will be emailed to you in 30 – 45 days. You will also receive many phone calls from Dunn & Bradstreet to verify your information and then they will try to solicit additional products for you to purchase. Some clients have even reported receiving calls on a daily basis!

We do not recommend obtaining a free D&B number. When you set this number up you will not obtain a duns rating. In place of your duns rating you will either have a "--" or a "DS." There are many lenders that will not lend money to your business unless you have the proper rating.

Option 2

D&B has something they call a "Credit Builder" program (currently $599.00). This service is only recommended if you have numerous vendors that you have accounts with that are not currently reporting to D&B. Their service calls your vendors to verify your account. Once D&B verifies the vendors, they will be added as trade references on your business credit file. D&B will allow you to add up to 6 references; you will have 30 days to add these. D&B is reputable and verifies information, so be sure to submit it correctly.

Some sales reps have gone as far as telling business owners that they will be "Black Listed" if they do not purchase this product and they will never be able to obtain business funding. This is not true.

Warning! What D&B will not tell you is that the references you give them to verify must be set up in the D&B system for more than one year in order to be added to your business credit file. Given the fact that most business owners are not set up with D&B, there is a good chance that many of your references will not be added. Therefore, most business owners will not need this service.

Option 3

There is a more preferable option to setting up your D&B number. D&B has another program (currently $299.00) with this program you will have an account representative to set up your initial file, make any changes or updates, and dispute any inaccuracies. You will also receive a proper D&B rating and your eUpdate password so you can log into your file and watch your business credit grow. We recommend that everyone purchase this program. Please contact us directly and we will give you our D&B account representative's name so you can deal directly with them.

It is also important that you do not advise D&B of your current position of being a part of a credit building service. This will cause them to flag your D-U-N-S® number and block trade accounts from being added to it. What and how you operate your business is private and you should not share unnecessary information with others. When you open accounts on the next step and place some small orders, you will want to be patient, as it may take over 30 days for those trade lines to be added to your profile.

D&B sells your good credit information to lenders, vendors, leasers and other credit grantors by calling and verifying business information on millions of businesses. They make their money by selling your information to businesses that might want to sell you products because of your good credit. Present yourself in the best light possible as far as having a professional website, professional employees, and in the volume of business that you do.

eUpdate Password

This password will provide you access to your credit file whenever you want to see it, 24 hours a day, seven days a week. D&B will allow you to update, change and remove certain information as well as view your company credit file for accuracy.

Please do not make any changes to your company profile unless you know exactly what you are doing. There is certain information that you will not want to provide to D&B and there are some changes which may have a negative effect on your file. Beware; do not eUpdate your file more than 2 times per 6 months. If you need to make changes, it is recommended that you work with your account representative. You should not log in to view your account excessively either, no more than 1 time per month to be safe.

You do need to ensure that everything is correct and

accurate. You will also enjoy watching your PAYDEX score increase as you continue to build business credit.

As you add trade accounts to your file, D&B will generate a PAYDEX score. This is similar to your personal FICO score in that the score statistically measures your business creditworthiness instead of personal creditworthiness.

A PAYDEX score of 80 is similar to that of a 700 personal FICO score. You will need a PAYDEX score of 75 to obtain favorable financing. To obtain a PAYDEX score, you will need at least five trade accounts reporting to your file. You will also want those accounts to report favorable payment history. If you pay your bills on time, they will. If you pay your bills late, your PAYDEX score will drop. Depending on how early or late you pay your bills, your PAYDEX score will adjust accordingly. If you pay early, then you can achieve a score that is over 80.

www.corporatecreditconcepts.com

Understanding Your D&B Report

The first thing you will want to look at is your overall D&B company rating. This is found at the top right hand side of the business credit report. If you have provided D&B with financials of your business, you will have a rating from 5A to HH. This score reflects your company's size based on your Net Worth or equity of the company. If you have released financials that show a negative net worth, your business will not be rated. It will show a "-" where the rating belongs.

The other half the report is your composite credit appraisal. This is a number from 1 to 4 that is listed next to your overall rating. The 1 through 4 rating reflects D&B's overall assessment of your company's creditworthiness. This number is based on your financials and payment history. One is the highest credit assessment that you can receive, while 4 is the lowest.

We suggest that you do not provide D&B with your financials. If you do not provide your financials then your rating will be a 1R or a 2R. The number represents the size of your business with 10 or more employees. The 2 represents a business with less than 10 employees. The R represents that they have not been provided with financials. After the R rating, your company will be assigned a composite credit appraisal between 2 and 4. Since no financials have been reported, they base the ranking on payment history, public filings and time in business. A 2 is the highest composite credit rating that you will receive without providing financial statements. A 1R2 and a 1R3 will be fine if you are looking for financing.

There are also other alternative ratings that D&B uses. These are used in special cases and for special industries such as a bank or insurance company.

An alternative rating that may be of interest is the DS rating. The DS stands for D-U-N-S® Support. This rating is applied to those companies who have provided information to D&B, but this information has not yet been verified. The DS rating is neither good nor bad; however, there are many lenders that will not lend money if you have this type of rating. This simply means that D&B does not have sufficient information to provide the business with a regular rating. The DS rating is more or less a marketing record that shows that the company is on their marketing list but a full investigation has not yet been performed.

The next score you will want to look at is your PAYDEX score. The PAYDEX score is a unique, dollar-weighted indicator. This provides an instant overview of how a firm has paid its bills in the past, and how the firm is likely to pay its bills in the future. This is a very important score when it comes to being approved for corporate credit financing.

The PAYDEX is a 1 to 100 weighted numerical score of payment performance. The score is calculated by using up to 875 payment experiences from the trade references reported to D&B. As you can see in the PAYDEX Score Key below, an 80 is considered a perfect PAYDEX score. If your payment terms to a vendor are 30 days net, then on the 30th day after billing your vendor has received your check, your payment is on time. Anything above 80 means that you actually paid before the due date and anything below means you paid some amount late. Most PAYDEX scores do not include anywhere near the 875 maximum payment experiences. You will need 5 trade accounts that report on your business to generate a PAYDEX score. Remember, anything above 75 is good.

There is another important aspect of the PAYDEX system that you need to know. This weighted average score gives more weight to the trade accounts that report higher amounts of credit extended and less weight to trade accounts that are reporting lower dollar amounts of credit.

Financial Strength		Composite Credit Appraisal			
Rating	$Revenue$	High	Good	Fair	limited
5A	50,000,000 and over	1	2	3	4
4A	10,000,000 to 49,999,999	1	2	3	4
3A	1,000,000 to 9,999,999	1	2	3	4
2A	750,000 to 999,999	1	2	3	4

1A	500,000 to 749,999	1	2	3	4
BA	300,000 to 499,999	1	2	3	4
BB	200,000 to 299,999	1	2	3	4
CB	125,000 to 199,999	1	2	3	4
CC	75,000 to 124,999	1	2	3	4
DC	50,000 to 74,999	1	2	3	4
DD	35,000 to 49,999	1	2	3	4
EE	20,000 to 34,999	1	2	3	4
FF	10,000 to 19,999	1	2	3	4
GG	5,000 to 9,999	1	2	3	4
HH	Up to 4,999	1	2	3	4

Rating Classification		Composite Credit Appraisal			
Rating					
1R	10 employees and over		2	3	4
2R	1 to 9 employees		2	3	4

Alternative Ratings Used	
INV	Indicates that D&B is currently conducting an investigation to gather information for a new report.

DS		Indicates that the information available does not permit D&B to classify the company within our rating key.
- (blank)		The blank symbol should not be interpreted as indicating that credit should be denied. It simply means that the information available to D&B does not permit us to classify the company within our rating key and that further enquiry should be made before reaching a decision. Some reasons for using a "-" symbol include: deficit net worth, bankruptcy proceedings, lack of insufficient payment information, or incomplete history information.
ER		Certain lines of business, primarily banks, insurance companies and government entities do not lend themselves to classification under the D&B Rating system. Instead, we assign these types of businesses an Employee range symbol based on the number of people employed. No other significance should be attached to this symbol. ERN should not be interpreted negatively. It simply means we do not have information indicating how many people are employed at this firm.
NQ		Not Quoted. This is generally assigned when a business has been confirmed as no longer active at the location, or when D & B is unable to confirm active operations. It may also appear on some branch reports, when the branch is located in the same city as the headquarters.

US Employee Range Designation	
ER1	1,000 or more employees
ER2	500 to 999 employees
ER3	100 to 499 employees
ER4	50 to 99 employees
ER5	20 to 49 employees
ER6	10 to 19 employees
ER7	5 to 9 employees
ER8	1 to 4 employees
ERN	Not Available

D&B Score Interpretation Table	
D&B PAYDEX Score	Payment Habit
100	Anticipate
90	Discount
80	Prompt
70	15 days beyond terms
60	22 days beyond terms
50	30 days beyond terms
40	60 days beyond terms
30	90 days beyond terms
20	120 days beyond terms
UN	Unavailable

www.corporatecreditconcepts.com

PAYDEX	PAYDEX Value Chart
	Average Days to Pay
100	30 days sooner than terms
99	29 days sooner than terms
98	28 days sooner than terms
97	27 days sooner than terms
96	26 days sooner than terms
95	25 days sooner than terms
94	24 days sooner than terms
93	23 days sooner than terms
91	22 days sooner than terms
90	21 days sooner than terms
89	28 days sooner than terms
88	16 days sooner than terms
87	14 days sooner than terms
86	12 days sooner than terms
85	10 days sooner than terms
84	8 days sooner than terms
83	6 days sooner than terms
82	4 days sooner than terms
81	2 days sooner than terms
80	**ON TERMS**
79	2 days beyond terms
78	3 days beyond terms
77	5 days beyond terms
76	6 days beyond terms
75	8 days beyond terms
74	9 days beyond terms
73	11 days beyond terms
72	12 days beyond terms
71	14 days beyond terms
70	15 days beyond terms
69	16 days beyond terms
68	17 days beyond terms
67	18 days beyond terms
66	19 days beyond terms
65	19 days beyond terms
64	19 days beyond terms
63	20 days beyond terms

62	21 days beyond terms
61	22 days beyond terms
60	22 days beyond terms
59	23 days beyond terms
58	24 days beyond terms
57	25 days beyond terms
56	26 days beyond terms
55	26 days beyond terms
54	27 days beyond terms
53	28 days beyond terms
52	29 days beyond terms
51	29 days beyond terms
50	30 days beyond terms
49	33 days beyond terms
48	36 days beyond terms
47	39 days beyond terms
46	42 days beyond terms
45	45 days beyond terms
44	48 days beyond terms
43	51 days beyond terms
42	54 days beyond terms
41	57 days beyond terms
40	60 days beyond terms
39	63 days beyond terms
38	66 days beyond terms
37	69 days beyond terms
36	72 days beyond terms
35	75 days beyond terms
34	78 days beyond terms
33	81 days beyond terms
32	84 days beyond terms
31	87 days beyond terms
30	90 days beyond terms
29	93 days beyond terms
28	96 days beyond terms
27	99 days beyond terms
26	102 days beyond terms
25	105 days beyond terms
24	108 days beyond terms

23	111 days beyond terms
22	114 days beyond terms
21	117 days beyond terms
20	120 days beyond terms
1 to 19	Over 120 days beyond terms

Financial Stress Score

The Financial Stress model predicts the probability of a firm stopping business without paying their creditors in full, then reorganizing to obtain relief from creditors under law over the next year. Scores are calculated statistically using a model that is derived from D&B's extensive data files.

Financial Stress Score (2001)			
Financial Stress Class	Financial Stress Score Range	Percentile Score Range	Incidence of Financial Stress
1	1377-1875	21-100	0.49%
2	1353-1376	11-20	1.37%
3	1303-1352	5-10	3.73%
4	1225-1302	2-4	8.30%
5	1001-1224	1	35.80%

"0" denotes an indication of open bankruptcy or out of business at the location. "0" may also denote higher risk situations.

The incidence of Financial Stress National Average for all firms in the US in D&B's file is 1.4%. The Incidence of Financial Stress shows the percentage of firms in a given Class that discontinues business over the past year with loss to creditors.

Commercial Credit Score

The US Commercial Credit Score predicts the possibility of a firm paying in a delinquent manner (90+ days) during the next year based on the information in D&B's file. The score is calculated using statistically valid models derived from D&B's extensive data files.

Commercial Credit Score			
Commercial Credit Score	Credit Score Percentile	Credit Score Class	Incidence of Delinquency
536-670	91-100	1	2.5%
493-535	71-90	2	4.8%

376-422	11-30	4	24.2%
101-375	1-10	5	58.8%

"0" generally denotes indication of open bankruptcy or out of business at the location. "0" may also denote higher risk situations.

Incidence of Delinquent Payment Assignment Table (2001)		
Minimum Score	Maximum Score	Incidence or Delinquent Payment
96	100	2.1%
91	95	2.9%
86	90	3.6%
81	85	4.4%
76	80	5.2%
66	70	7.3%
61	65	8.7%
56	60	10.5%
51	55	12.2%
46	50	13.9%
41	45	15.5%

36	40	17.2%
31	35	18.4%
26	30	20.2%
16	20	24.6%
11	15	29.6%
6	10	44.9%
1	5	72.7%

The Incidence of Delinquent Payment for all firms in the US in D&B's file is 17.3%.

The Incidence of Delinquent Payment shows the percentage of firms in a given percentile range that paid in a delinquent manner (90+ days) over the past 12 months. The Incidence of Delinquent Payment among all firms in the D&B's files represents the national delinquency rate.

D&B Score Interpretation Table	
D&B PAYDEX Score	Payment Habit
100	Anticipate
90	Discount
80	Prompt
70	15 days beyond terms
60	22 days beyond terms
50	30 days beyond terms
40	60 days beyond terms
30	90 days beyond terms
20	120 days beyond terms
UN	Unavailable

*Charts and graph taken directly from D&B site.

Trade Credit

Trade credit is credit that a business receives from a particular vendor. It may also be called "vendor credit." When you set up an account with a vendor, be certain that they invoice your business. You need a net 30 account. This means that you have 30 days to pay for the merchandise that you have ordered.

Once you pay (early or on time) the vendor reports to

the business credit bureaus. This allows the vendor to become a trade reference. This is important because you need five trade accounts to generate your PAYDEX score. Experian only requires two trade accounts.

I need to stress that the vendors we refer you to are very important. These are vendors that will report your payment to the business credit bureaus. The majority of vendors do not report your payment history, so it does no good for you to do business with them because you are not getting credit for payments you make on time.

Make sure that you choose trade companies that are set up with net 30 and revolving terms and most importantly, report to the credit bureaus.

What happens if the trade account is not reporting to D&B? This does happen on occasion, but it is generally easy to remedy. All you have to do is call the vendor and ask that they report your payment history. Many vendors will report for individual businesses. If they still do not report your payment history, then you should send a letter including each of your payments. The letter should request that they report the information to the business credit bureaus. The letter should include:

- ✓ Company's Name
- ✓ Address
- ✓ Phone Number
- ✓ D-U-N-S® Number
- ✓ Experian file number
- ✓ Account number for vendor

Experian and Equifax do not publish how they figure their business credit scores. However, if you always pay your bills on time, stay away from collections and high debt, then your Experian and Equifax scores will be favorable.

How are Corporate Experian and Equifax set up?

You are unable to set-up your Experian and Equifax business credit files yourself. This must be done by your vendor trade accounts that are reporting your payment information to the bureaus. Because it is set-up this way, it is important that your vendor credit information is 100% correct. The vendors use the information you provide them and then report to the bureaus. If your information is incorrect, then the information reported will be incorrect. If your information is wrong, then it will show up on your credit file.

It is a very good idea to become personally familiar with these reports. You will also want to view them yourself on occasion. It is important to set-up accounts with businesses that report so that your information is reported. If not, you won't be able to develop a business credit file.

Chapter 6

What Do You Do After You Have Received Money from the Bank?

The money that we help you borrow is just a starting point. I cannot stress this enough. This is not the end, but just the beginning of the credit building process. Now that you have obtained credit, you need to use it and repay on time. You need to keep good deposits in your bank account so that the lines will continue to grow. Every 6 months, you can go back to the bank and ask for a line increase and an interest rate decrease. If you use your funds responsibly, then you can show a need for additional funds and the bank will lend it to you.

It is important to understand that, in most cases, we have obtained funding without the strong score that you are going to be building. The next step for you to take is to build trade credit and vendor relationships.

You don't want to stop the credit building at this point. If you continue to build business credit, you will be able to grow the initial amount that we helped you obtain. Many people see the funding that they have received as the end result and think that is all that needs to be done. This is not so. In fact, it's the complete opposite. This is a starting point for you.

You want to continue building business credit and setting up your trade credit because it will build a good business credit score. Remember, the business credit bureaus sell your information, which can provide you with more opportunities. As you continue to raise your credit score, the lender will go to the business credit bureaus and will purchase your information from those companies. As you build your rating and score, your information will begin to be included in the lists that they purchase.

Lenders purchase these lists to solicit businesses in good credit standing. They will begin to mail out "pre-approval" letters and other offers that may interest you. The better your score and rating is, the more frequent and better the offers you will receive. The lenders look at those businesses with good scores because they are considered to be more stable and a lower risk.

It is imperative that you also know that your Experian and Equifax business credit file is also set up through your trade accounts. Typically, lenders will look at D&B if they extend trade credit or vendor credit. Lenders who offer lines of credit, equipment financing, etc. may also look at Experian or Equifax.

The stronger your trade references are, the stronger your business credit scores will be. This combination of scores and ratings with the business credit bureaus will allow you to receive the best offers for additional financing.

Business Credit Cards

Business credit cards can be very useful in establishing additional financing options for your business. These are often the cheapest funds that you borrow. These credit card companies will also send out promotional checks, similar to personal credit cards. These checks may differ depending on the credit card company, but a good example is 3.9% interest for the life of the loan or 0% for 6 months, depending on the promotion that the company is offering at the time.

These are actual credit cards as well. These are not Office Max, Lowe's, or Staples credit cards that can only be used at their store. These credit cards are affiliated with Visa or MasterCard and therefore, can be used anywhere, not just at specific stores.

Once you have set up and finished the three previous steps for trade credit, you can apply for these business credit cards. Remember, the more credit you have with higher limits, the higher the limit you will obtain when applying for additional business cards. If you wait and build up higher limits, then you can receive even higher limits later on down the road.

If you go to the right credit card companies they will pull your business credit file first. If it is strong enough, then they will extend you credit without pulling your personal credit report. If you have built your business credit properly, it will be strong enough that you may not have to personally guarantee the card. This is something to look for in a business credit card application because there is often a clause that states you will have to pay the card personally if your business fails to do so.

Many credit card companies won't report to the credit bureaus. This is both bad and good. It is bad because you are not building trade references on your account. It is good because some credit cards won't like that your business has a lot of available credit. If they don't report on your personal file or your business file, then the next time that you apply, they won't even know that you have other accounts.

Personal Credit Inquiries

Many credit card companies will only pull from one personal credit bureau. This is an inquiry. If you call around for quotes, be sure to ask which bureau they pull. You can actually apply for 3 separate cards and only show one inquiry. For example, if Citibank pulls Equifax, American Express pulls TransUnion and Visa pulls Experian, then you can essentially apply and obtain three cards with only one inquiry with each bureau.

Clients often ask if we are able to send them to additional banks. The answer is yes and no. The reason we do not send you to a large number of banks is because they will all make inquiries on your personal credit report. This will lower your credit score slightly with each inquiry. By the time you go to the 5th or 6th bank, they will notice that several other banks have pulled your report. This makes them wonder about you and may be leery of lending you additional funds.

If you are interested in more financing, our coaches can send you to three of our banking contacts. Once you apply at those three banks, you can contact a credit restoration agency and have those inquiries removed. Once those are off your credit report, then you can apply at three more banks. When those banks pull your credit report, they will not see the inquiries and they may extend your business more funding. We can do this over and over again.

Business Lines of Credit

Another strategy that many clients have had success with is to take a business line of credit, for example, take $30,000 and deposit $10,000 in three separate banks. After that money is deposited you can go back to each bank where the money was deposited and apply for a business line of credit. After you have money deposited into the account and established a good average balance they will often offer higher amounts.

If each bank extended your business a $40,000 line of credit, you have just used your original $30,000 to increase your total amount of business credit to $150,000. ($30,000 + $40,000 x 3 banks = $150,000)

Do not open more than 3 bank accounts within a 90-day period of time. If you do, then your business may get caught in the ChexSystems.

If this strategy is of interest to you, contact us and we will direct you to the appropriate banks.

Equipment Leasing

Once you have had a $40,000 loan for six months, you will be able to get an equipment lease for about $80,000. Leasing companies will typically approve an amount that is double the bank loan.

If you pay them both off on time and hold them for six months, you can go back to the bank and request a credit line increase of $20,000. This will provide you with $60,000, at which time you can also ask for a lower interest rate. The bank will see if you have "comparable credit," the $80,000 lease. They may then approve your line increase. After six months, you can go back and ask for more. As long as you show you can service the debt and have a need for the money, the banks will continue to look at lending you more money. You should do this step by step over a two year period at intervals of every six months. This allows you to build a large credit line and the ability to be able to be approved for even higher equipment leases.

You can apply a similar concept to your business credit card balances. Start with a small line and pay it on time. After six months, use the card to try and buy something over the limit. If you are turned down, ask to speak to a credit representative and ask for an increase. If you have been paying on time, then you should be approved for an increase in your credit line.

Because you have continued to obtain business credit cards with higher limits, you will be able to build excellent business credit card scores and your mail box will be busting with credit card offers.

Remember; if you overdo it, you can begin to hurt your business credit score the same way you can hurt your personal score.

Chapter 7

Maintaining Your D&B Report

Once your report is set-up and you have a high PAYDEX score, you will want to be certain that you continually maintain your report. Check your report periodically. You may want to consider purchasing the Monitoring Service that D&B offers. This service allows you to receive alerts either positive or negative on your report. There are several areas that you will be notified of if they change including:

- ✓ Credit Rating
- ✓ Suits, liens or judgments on your business
- ✓ PAYDEX score changes
- ✓ Changes to financial statements
- ✓ Other significant news involving your business

Find Out Who is Reporting On Your Business

Many business owners find that they have a low PAYDEX score when they receive their Business

Information Report from D&B. It may lead them to scratch their heads and wonder why, even when they are paying their bills on time.

You won't be able to find out which companies are reporting negative information to your file as D&B does not tell businesses this information. You will, however, be able to obtain a list of all the companies that are reporting to your file. Upon request, you will get an alphabetical list of each company that is reporting to the business credit bureau as well as a number of times they reported.

If you'd like to see this list, call your D&B representative and asked them for the list of companies reporting on your business. There must be five or more companies reporting for your Representative to be able to pull this list. Once you get your report, turn to page 2. You'll find an overview of the companies that have reported the dollar weighted payments and your PAYDEX score. The companies will be sorted by supplier industry.

If you have less than 20 companies on your list, your D&B representative might choose to simply read the list to you over the phone. On one side you will see the total number of companies in your DB file and on the other side you'll see the total received. You can request that your D&B representative e-mail you the information. If you do, you should receive the file within 24 to 48 hours. There are times when you may not receive the report, so make sure you follow up with your Representative and tell them if you've already made a request.

Other information that you will find on this report are the total dollar amount that all of the trades reported to your account, the highest credit, which is the single largest amount that any one trade has reported. The terms will show the percentage of payments that have been made to the top 10 industries.

Chapter 8

Correcting Information on Your D&B Report

Nearly every D&B report contains some errors, so don't be alarmed if you do review your report and find an error of two. Later in the chapter we will discuss how we can fix those errors. We'll also show you how you can avoid being flagged as a high risk or put on the fraud list. Most problems that need resolution will be dealt with through the eUpdate website; however, any major issues need special attention. In those cases it's best to pay D&B to get an account representative to fix the problem quickly and efficiently so that it does not affect your file.

Under your D-U-N-S® number, you will find your company name. Make sure that what is shown on the report is the exact legal name you have listed for your business. For instance, if you are an LLC, make sure it is there. If you have a DBA (Doing Business As), make sure it is listed there directly under your business name. All business detail must be accurate. If your mailing address is not listed exactly as it is on your business license, you need to make the correction. This will make sure that all your information is going to the right account.

To update your file, click on "Establish and Manage Company Profile" at the bottom of D&B website. You will then be able to log into the eUpdate. Click on "Update Only." Much of your company information will already be filled in. All you need to do is make corrections to the information that is wrong.

About Your Company

This is where all the information about your company resides. If any details, such as name, address, phone number, and mailing address, are incorrect, you would make the change here. If you are making a change to your business name, you must remember to check either the Name Correction -- Misspelled box, or the Legal Name Change box.

Anytime you legally change the name of your business, you need to provide legal documentation from the Secretary of State so that you can prove it. A legal name change is not the same as change in ownership. If this is not clear, D&B may misinterpret the information and change your "control date", which will then re-list you as a new business. That will be like starting from square one and you will again have difficulty trying to obtain financing over $25,000. It is imperative that you remember to check the box "This is a correction." To make sure the change is dealt with properly, it is best to have an account representative make the change.

If ownership has remained the same but you have changed the structure of the business, you'll want to check the box "This is a correction". Changing from an LLC to a corporation can sometimes be misconstrued as a "control change". At that point, a bank may misinterpret this change and view your company as a new business. And the past history you have built with a lender will then be erased. So as you can see, making sure that errors are corrected properly is vital to the continued growth of your business credit score.

Any changes that you make to this file should be taken seriously. Once the changes are made it is best to review them to make sure they were done correctly. Once you have clicked on the "Submit My eUpdate" icon, these changes will be forwarded to D&B. Follow-up the next day by checking you report to make sure the changes show.

You will not be able to make any more updates until the first updates have been completed. Sometimes a representative from D&B will contact you to make sure that the information that has been input into the file is correct.

About Your Ownership

Your company's ownership information will be listed in the next section. You can update this information online as well, but before you make any changes remember that the amount of time you've been in business directly affects your credit scoring. Lenders look very heavily at this section so be careful when you make changes as they will have an impact on whether or not you are able to receive financing.

Pay particular attention to how you make the change. For instance, is the change simply a correction of information? Or did some important information actually change? You may have the CEO of your company listed as David Johnson. But in reality, his name is David Johnston. This would be a correction. But if you change the CEO of your company from David Johnson to Robert Johnson because the CEO actually changed, D&B will note this as a "control change". If that happens you may be listed as a new business and your business credit will be wiped clean. As you can see, making sure that you are checking the appropriate box is important.

When in doubt, it is faster and much easier to have an account representative make changes to your file to ensure that your business credit file is not harmed.

Please contact us if you need any help or are unsure

about what changes you can make on your D&B report.

About Management

All the information in the previous section regarding ownership of the company and the percentage of ownership when more than one owner is involved will be verified. eUpdate will use the terms "principals" and "owner/officers" even if that is not the case in your particular company. But in this section, you will be filling in the information regarding management and list the people you want to include in the report plus their responsibilities in the company.

How do you decide who to include? Anyone who is working in your company that is an expert or is considered well known in your field of business should be included if they are in your employment. Their knowledge and reputation could help your business reputation.

The owner and CEO of the business isn't the only person who can update the report. You can choose another individual in your company to do the task by giving them your D-U-N-S® number and eUpdate password. Any person who is listed on the report can contact customer service, if need be, to update or dispute information on the report with D&B. This is not unexpected since all credit card company customer service departments will only speak with the person on the account record and only after they've verified the account details. This ensures the integrity of the account and prevents fraudulent changes.

 Make sure that the people you have chosen to be on your credit bureau record are trustworthy. Employees such as your CFO, office manager or bookkeeper are good to have on the list as they have specific knowledge of your financial dealings. As an added safeguard, make sure you pass this book to them so that they can come up to speed on what you are trying to accomplish with your business credit account.

Make sure you let all personnel on the D&B list that you do not want to divulge financial information to

D&B. There may be times when a D&B representative will ask for information; however, it is your right not to give that information away.

Think of it this way. Do you want your competitor to have access to all your financial records? My guess is no! By giving this information to D&B, you are opening your accounting department for the business world to see because D&B uses this information to sell lists to other businesses.

You must always keep in mind the role that D&B is playing for you. You need a good score to get financial backing from lenders. They need as much information about you to make money by selling your information to others. Hold your cards close to your chest and don't give them that information.

About Your Operations

The business operations section is the last section where you will make changes regarding your area of business, your number of employees, facility information and your sales revenues.

At the top of the report you will put in a description of your business. Underneath that you'll enter your standard industrial classification code or SIC. This code shows what type of business you are in.

Make sure you check that the number of employees listed on the report is correct. You'll want to make sure you are put into the proper rating. For instance, if you have less than 10 employees you'll receive a 2R rating. More than 10 employees will give you a 1R rating.

The next section will cover your sales revenues, types of customers you have, your payment terms and the number of accounts you have. You don't want to be broadcasting this type of information so be careful to keep this information confidential. Simple sales revenues are fine if you don't mind your competition knowing. Lenders will want this information when you apply for credit, but you can give it to them directly.

One exception is if you are looking to obtain financing

from a lender that requires $1,000,000 or more in sales revenues. You may want to include this information if your annual sales revenue is higher. If it is not higher, consider using a projected income amount for the coming year.

You'll need to identify whether you are working in a residential or commercial area in the last section and whether you rent or own the facility you use for business. Sometimes a lender will also want information about square footage of your facility.

Once all the information is correct, hit the submit button at the bottom of the page. As mentioned earlier, you don't want to make changes on a regular basis. This will be a red flag for D&B and your account could end up with "special event" language added to the profile. Too many changes could look like you're trying to manipulate your report and you may have the note "there have been a high number of updates at the request of the principal on the report" added to your file. Make a note of your last update and collect data to change until a fair amount of time has passed when you can update it all at once.

The number of times you log into your account is monitored by D&B and can also be a red flag for lenders. One of our clients was decline funding by a bank for this reason. This client told us she'd only logged in a couple of times, however, in checking we found that she'd logged in over 139 times in one month! This is way too often and ended up harming her. Don't let it happen to you.

If all you have are a few changes to be made, you can do this yourself. If you have a lot of changes to be made, sometimes it can take a while for the new data to show up in your file. Sometimes it doesn't show up at all. If you have a lot of information that needs changing, it's best to have an account representative at D&B make the changes for you. The process will go much smoother that way and you can always follow up with your representative if the information is not changed.

Chapter 9

How To Raise Your PAYDEX Score

One of the most important sections of your D&B Business Credit Report is the payment summary section. There are two scores in this section that are critical to the report and can separate a good report from a bad report. While the two scores, the PAYDEX score and the PAYDEX score key, are related, they deal with separate issues that you need to know and understand.

PAYDEX Score

How timely you pay your bills factors into your PAYDEX score and is a good indicator to lenders of how you are going to pay your bills in the future. Lenders look at this score carefully when deciding whether or not to give out a loan. You'll need at least 5 trade accounts reporting to your file to get a

www.corporatecreditconcepts.com

PAYDEX score, but the score itself is calculated by using as much as 875 payments.

I've included a D&B PAYDEX score key chart below for your reference. Getting a PAYDEX score key of 80 means you have a perfect score. When you pay all your bills on time, meaning on or before the due date, you'll get a perfect score. Remember, to get this score, you need to have 5 trade references reporting to D&B on your company.

D&B PAYDEX Score Key	
100	Anticipate
90	Discount
80	Prompt
70	Slow to 15 Days
60	Slow to 22 Days
50	Slow to 30 Days
40	Slow to 60 Days
30	Slow to 90 Days
20	Slow to 120 Days

A PAYDEX score is a weighted average. That means that the higher the dollar amount that is reported, the more weight the report gives it in terms of giving you a score. For instance, if your company made one late payment over 60 days on a bill for $50 and another one for $50,000 on time, more weight is given to the trade report that was for $50,000 and your rating will be good. However, if you have 10 $50 bills that you paid on time and 1 $50,000 bill that you paid late, it will affect your score and you will have a bad PAYDEX rating score.

Most lenders are comfortable extending credit to businesses with a PAYDEX score of 75 or above. Having a PAYDEX score below 70 will mean you will have trouble getting financing. A score below 65 will almost certainly mean you'll be automatically declined for credit.

D&B has a trade reporting program available to businesses to help collect the payment experiences involved in determining a PAYDEX score. You need to have at least 500 credit experiences added to your report on a yearly basis to qualify for this program. Over 6,100 businesses and 300 banks participate in the trade reporting program. All of the 315,000,000 payment experiences that D&B collects each year are downloaded from the participating companies accounts receivable systems into the D&B database. It is then verified to make sure the information is accurate. The normal cycle for payment history is 16 months. After that amount of time has passed, it is deleted.

With the sheer volume of payment histories it might seem logical that most of your suppliers would be reporting data, however, this is not the case. A small number of companies report to D&B and therefore represents only a small number of what is part of a larger picture. One look at your report and you will see that it doesn't represent all your business payments over a 16 month period.

You need to take a two-sided approach toward changing your PAYDEX score. The first task is to remove all negative reports from your report. You will then want to increase the number of positive reports as well as the amount of each report. One or two trade references that are negative is all it takes to lower your score, so removing them can make an immediate change.

By looking at the list of companies that report to your account, you can determine which company is causing you problems. For instance, if you know that you've had a few payments late to one company and it is listed on your report, then chances are those late payments have affected your score in a negative way. Your next step is to remedy that problem by either paying on time or, if they are reporting your payments incorrectly, get them to correct the error.

Sometimes these problems are easy to remedy. If you have the wrong payment address in your file and your payment has to pass through several hands before it gets to the right desk, the company may be marking your payment as being late even though it reached them in time. If so, you'll need to update your records to make sure your payments are being sent to the appropriate address. You might have set up special payment terms with a vendor, but that information has not been passed down correctly to their accounting department, causing them to flag your payment as late even though it has been paid within the agreed upon time. If so, check it out and make sure that all parties involved are on board with the payment terms that you have negotiated.

Sometimes you may be in negotiations over a particular shipment or the replacement of damage goods or even a credit for damaged goods. If that's the case, perhaps the payment or accounting was handled incorrectly. If you should have had a credit and D&B shows an outstanding payment due, you need to dispute the report to get it corrected.

You must pick your battles though. Make sure you are really in the right when making a dispute as a dispute that turns out that the trade is right and you are wrong, the reference will stay on your report for another 16 months. Therefore, if you find something that is 14 or 15 months old, no matter if you are right or wrong, it's best to leave it alone as the negative reference will be dropped from your report soon. At that point, the risk of having a negative reference on your report for another 16 months is not worth it.

Don't try to handle a dispute on your own. Call your account representative with D&B and tell them you want to dispute a trade reference. D&B will recheck with the trade reference. Every time you speak to someone at D&B, make sure you get their name and number so you can call them back to follow up. If you have a few references to dispute, you'll only be able to dispute 3 at a time, so make sure you choose them wisely and make sure you are disputing the largest charges as resolving them will give you the best chance of changing your PAYDEX score.

When D&B contacts the company that is reporting your payments late, one of 3 things will happen.
1. The trade reference will come back and inform D&B that their files are correct and the reference will remain on your report for another 16 months.
2. The trade will re-report with the current status, replacing the information with new information.
3. The trade reference doesn't respond to D&B

Obviously, your goal is number 2 or 3. Why? D&B will give the trade reference 15 days to respond. If they do not respond after 15 days, the negative reference is removed from your report, thereby helping to increase your PAYDEX score.

Many times, if the trade reference plans to confirm or supply new details, it will happen within a week of D&B contacting them. Make sure you follow up with your account representative at D&B so that if the trade reference does not respond, the negative report is removed.

Once the 15 days is up and the account representative has dealt with the responses or non-responses appropriately, you will be able to dispute 3 more references. By checking and challenging the references that you believe are wrong, you can help to ensure your PAYDEX score is good.

Let's talk about the historical PAYDEX. When you request a free report online, you will only get the most current information. Any past information over the last year will not be listed. However, D&B can produce different historical reports for you.

Why is this important? When you make a dispute on a reference, it will only change the current report, not the historical report. Because of this, you'll need to request that your account representative work toward removing the old incorrect data as well, as the old data will continue to appear on any historical reports you request. While you're at it, it couldn't hurt to have positive information added to your report.

Your D&B account representative might try to sell you D&B's Payment Investigation Service for $499. If you only have a few vendors to report or remove, it won't be worth the money. However, your goal is to get a score higher than 70, which can happen when you delete negative information. But to make your score higher, you'll need more positive trade reference information to offset the ones that were deleted. Using this service can help you increase your score.

While you only need 5 trade references reporting to

get a good score, those 5 trade reference need to report positively. If they aren't, you'll need more than 5 trade references reporting with positive information. For every 5 trade references you add to the report, you will be charged and additional $499. Make sure you are following the rules for adding references before you send the information to your account representative.

Once you have 5-7 references that are qualified, contact each of them and let them know that D&B will be contacting them for verification. You'll want to let them know the kind of information D&B is looking for so they don't inadvertently give information that can be misconstrued by D&B.

For instance, if their normal terms are net 30 and you've negotiated to pay net 60 and have been paying consistently every 55 days, it could cause problems with D&B. If the vendor tells D&B this, even though the vendor doesn't look at you as being late, D&B will see if that way as you will be paying 25 days later than their normal business terms. So make sure you relay exactly what information D&B is looking for and why they need verification so it doesn't cause a black mark against you.

Any references you have can be phoned in, mailed or faxed to D&B. If you have a few extra references, all the better. Some of your references may not qualify and you'll only need to go out and get more.

Your account representative, if you've been working with one, will probably send you a Payment Investigation Service form, which you need to fill out with all the reference information you have and submit to D&B. The form is also available on the website when you log into eUpdate. It will take D&B 15 days to verify all your references, no matter how many references you supply.

Percentage of Payments Within Terms

Located beneath your PAYDEX score, the Percentage of Payments within Terms measures just that, how many payments you've made within the agreed upon timeframe provided by your references.

Unlike the PAYDEX score, this score is not affected by dollar amount. Each payment is weighted equally. To reach an acceptable level, you need to have a score of 60-65%. Higher is much better and if you are over 70% you are considered to have an excellent percentage.

Let's break down the score by type. Ten $50 trades reporting on time and 1 $100,000 trade report late would give you a score of 91%. However, putting those same numbers into play would give you a much lower PAYDEX score because the $100,000 payment made late would be given much heavier standing. The same would be true if you were late with 10 $50 trade references and on time with 1 $100,000 trade reference.

Of course, removing any negatives references, as mentioned earlier, will make your scores higher. When at all possible, try to remove any negative references to increase your score.

For instance, if you have a percentage of payments

within terms listed as 50% and a PAYDEX score of 70 with 10 trades reporting, this will be a problem for you. This means that you have 5 trade references reporting you on time and 5 reporting you late. You'll need to add 5 trade references that report you as being on time to increase your score to an acceptable level of 65%. Using the Payment Investigation Service for $449 will help you achieve this.

Sometimes it's better to wait it out for a few months, unless you really need to change your score quickly to obtain financing. Some of your negative reference reports may drop off the report and you'll be able to get a higher score without having to spend the money.

Maintaining Your Scores

As you can see, it will take some work and persistence not only to get your score where you want it to be, but to keep it there. Make sure you continue to pay the trades that are reporting to D&B on time to prevent a fluctuation in your scores.

Business has fluctuations and sometimes it is not always possible to pay early or on time. If this happens, make sure you have another vendor you can add to the list to help offset any negative references. If you are working with a new vendor, find out if they report to D&B. There are benefits for vendors when they report as well.

Chapter 10

How to Remove Negative Items from Your Credit Report

You may see some negative items on your report, such as collections, judgments and liens. These reporting's will impact your PAYDEX score in a negative way and you'll want to make sure you remove them.

How to Remove Collection Items from Your Report

Any collection item that shows you've paid 120 days or more late will a have devastating effect on your PAYDEX score, especially if that reporting is for a large dollar amount. Many times there will also be unfavorable comments with the reporting and you'll want to have both removed from your report as they affect not only your PAYDEX score but your D&B rating as well. Lenders do not like to see comments such as "Bad Debt" or "Credit Refused" on a report because it is a red flag that they should not do business with you.

These negative references and comments will be broken down into categories by dollar weight in the Other Payment Categories section. The Unfavorable Comment section will give you the number of items in each category. The section for Collection may give you a dollar amount for each item. Each section will have a payment history where you can see the items listed with unfavorable comments and items placed for collections.

We'll start with items placed for collections, since they are easier to deal with. D&B customer service can provide you with all the information needed to find out which company placed you for collection along with the file name and collector's name. Make sure you also get the name and number of the account representative at D&B so you can follow up with them later, if need be.

Disputing a collection reference is similar to disputing

a trade reference. Tell the account representative that you'd like to dispute the report even if one of the three things apply.

1. You have never heard of the company before.
2. You know the company but are either not making payments, have paid it off or are in the process of paying.
3. You are disputing a charge because the vendor was wrong and incorrectly billed you.

The D&B account representative will handle the dispute in the same manner as a trade reference reporting and one of the following things will happen.

1. The trade responds and says that the information is correct.
2. The trade responds and the information is incorrect.
3. The trade does not respond at all.

Like with a trade reference dispute, if the trade does not respond within 15 days, the entry is wiped clean from the file. If the information is incorrect, it will be removed as well. However, if number 1 occurs, you will have to delve deeper to see where you are at with the payment.

If you've paid the debt in full, it will remain on your report until the company requests that D&B delete it from the file. While that may seem like a bad thing, you can use this information to negotiate business terms with your vendor. Have them put in their terms that they will request any bad credit/collection information be removed from your D&B report when the issue is resolved. Only the person who puts the collection filing on your report can remove it, so it must be done by the company who placed you for collection. If it is not in your business terms that they will remove the collection reporting from you file, you can always ask them, especially if you have had a good relationship with them in the past.

If you do not have a good working relationship with this vendor or if the vendor is not one that you will be working with in the future, you can dispute the report.

Many vendors never respond to the D&B inquiry regarding a reporting, therefore, it is likely the collection information will be removed within 15 days anyway.

If you have a legitimate reason for not making payment to a particular trade, then you must present supporting documentation to D&B explaining why the reference is erroneous and why you are not paying the bill. You may mail or fax the information and they will work toward solving the problem. This move is effective because the worst that can happen is that the record will be changed to "payment history unknown" in which case it will not change your PAYDEX or D&B rating negatively.

There are times when it is hard to figure out what item is under collection. If it is listed as "other", there is no information to work with. You'll need to decipher who it is by looking at your list and doing a process of elimination.

If you do figure out which vendor reported the

collection, you must negotiate a settlement and ask for the negative information to be removed from the report. Most companies will be responsive; however, if they are not, you can always dispute the report.

How to Remove Financial Statements from Your Report

As previously mentioned, you do not want D&B to be posting your financial data, unless you have strong financials to show, and you don't mind making them public. If they are doing this, you'll want to take steps to have it removed. D&B wants this information and will call your bookkeeper, CPA or managers of your company to get it. You must make all your business partners aware that you do not want financial information to go to D&B, even though D&B will sound very convincing in their plight to obtain this data.

The conversation may go something like this:

"Mr. Owner, we have noticed that your financial information has not been updated recently. You need to send us your most current financial statement for

our file."

The account representative may even tell your team member that something bad will happen if the information isn't updated. This is not true. Make sure that everyone knows that unless they have specific permission from you, they should not be giving out financial information.

The only reason D&B wants this information is so that they can sell it with your credit report. This is bad news if your financials show that you are in the negative as you will not be approved for financing or leasing. It only takes one financial statement to wreak havoc on your financial options.

If this does happen to you and your financials are listed on your D&B report, you can fix this problem easily and it will only take about a week. Simply fax D&B and request that the information be removed immediately. If after two days the information is still there, send another fax. You should see your rating change from 2R to 1R, depending on how many employees you have.

If you have more than one department that reported financial data, then you may only see a partial removal of the information. Make sure you send a fax in for all departments that reported data.

Authors update: Given the current credit crunch there is a benefit to posting financial statements that one may want to consider now. If you don't mind having your company's financial statement open for public view then the benefit to posting them is, when applying for financing, banks or other lenders will get a better picture for your overall business and its ability to service the debt load. I would only recommend posting financials if (1) you are comfortable making this information public and (2) your financial are in very good shape. There is nothing worse than posting financials only to show your business is in turmoil.

How to Remove Suits, Liens and Judgments

If you have any suits, liens, bankruptcy, UCC filings or judgments against you, you will find that information under the public filing section of your report. This information is added after routine checking of public databases at the county, state and federal level and D&B will crosscheck to make sure the information they list is accurate.

However, there are times when a filing is inaccurate and you must be able to prove this if you are to have it deleted from the file. Any proving documentation about settlements, satisfactions or releases from the court or taxing authority will suffice in helping to prove the inaccuracy of the listing. Make sure you keep good records as these items could appear long after the judgment or settlement has been made, especially if the settlement was made out of court.

Even if you do settle it out of court, make sure there is a record of the settlement on file with the court in some official capacity. Filing a Stipulation of Dismissal or a Satisfaction of Judgment will be enough; however, it is always good to keep copies of the paperwork as well in case D&B does not get their information from the courthouse.

The courthouse record should have a docket number, case number or lien release number. Match that number with your paperwork and keep it on file. With this matching information you can fax a request with your information to D&B's Public Records Department at 610-807-1677. As long as you supply the proper documentation, D&B will remove the record. Follow up to make sure it has been taken care of and *removed* from your report, not just listed as *satisfied*. Even a satisfied or settled status on your report can have an effect.

If you don't have the proper paperwork, call customer service and talk to a representative, telling them you have an open suit, lien, etc. on your report, however, you do not have the paperwork for it because the data is old. D&B will then go back to the courthouse and check with a court clerk to verify the current status. This can be a long process and take up to 3 months to research if you settled out of court and didn't file a Stipulation of Dismissal or Satisfaction of Judgment on the item. This is just one more reason to make sure you keep good records and file all your settlements with the courthouse.

If you have an ongoing problem that is in the process of being resolved, ask the vendor to contact D&B with the status. Once the item has been satisfied, you can request that it be removed.

UCC Filings

The Public Filings Section of your report will also include any UCC filings that your company has had. All states enacted a UCC or Uniform Commercial Code to perfect a security interest in certain collateral. For instance, if you lease something, a UCC-1 is filed, showing "title" or a security interest in the lease. Once the lease period is satisfied, the leasing company should release this UCC-1 filing and transfer ownership to the lessee.

Having a UCC filing is neither good or bad, but they can be seen as positive because it shows the faith of other vendors in giving your company secured interest in a piece of collateral. New vendors will see you as a lower risk and can check with the past vendor to get a reference of how you paid for your lease.

One word of caution. If you have several UCC filings in a recent time frame, it could be viewed negatively as it may seem as though you are over extended. A lender may be weary of allowing you to take on more debt.

UCC filings will stay on your report for 5 years or less depending on the term of the lease. A lender should file a UCC-2 to remove the filing from your report. Whether you want the filings removed or not is up to you. If you have too many, then perhaps having some of them removed will show you in a more favorable light. Anything that has been terminated should stay on your report.

Bankruptcy

Unlike personal bankruptcy, a business bankruptcy can stay on your report for 25 years. Most lenders are weary of dealing with companies showing a bankruptcy and won't even consider working with you. However, if you had a personal bankruptcy and it shows on your report, you can fax a request to the Public Filings Department to have the bankruptcy language removed.

It's not so easy when the company was the one to file the bankruptcy. Bankruptcies are public record and D&B is not required to remove this information, even at your request, because it is accurate and pertains to their business dealings.

If ownership of the company changed after the bankruptcy, you can have the old data removed; however, you must prove the change of ownership. Send a fax and provide this information to D&B.

You're ultimate goal is to have your Public Filings Section blank to show the best business credit report possible. If you can't keep this section blank, then at least work toward showing them all satisfied. Maintaining good business credit is vital to the success of your business. You do not want to be declined credit before you even get your business off the ground.

Chapter 11

Advanced Strategies for Building Business Credit

CD Deposit Program: Business Funding Without a Personal Guarantee

The CD deposit program is very simple. We arrange deposits to be made at acceptable financial institutions worldwide, specifically Jumbo CD's ($100,000). The deposits we arrange cannot be encumbered, pledged, put in jeopardy, used to collateralize your loan, or used to guarantee your loan.

Our product makes your capital-seeking campaign easier and provides incentive for the lender to fund your package. Attaching our product to your loan package, line of credit request, or business project will make your capital-seeking proposal more appealing to your lender. In fact, our product provides more than just motivation for your lender to fund your project. Our product may provide the lender with liquidity for your loan and other loans. Your loan, line of credit, or borrowing package will stand out with our product attached to it. We even find the banks for you!

Our CD deposit program mandates a minimum of double your funding request amount in CD's be arranged for purchase at your lending financial institution. For example - imagine your funding request is $1,000,000. Your minimum amount of CD's arranged for transfer would be $2,000,000. Many bankers will look more favorably at your funding request when it is associated with such a large quantity of CD's purchased at their bank. Our minimum deposit amount is $100,000 and there is no maximum.

If you would like to obtain your funding request without a personal guarantee then we recommend that you deposit four times your funding request.

Increasing Credit Lines

Once you have a bank loan, for say $20,000, and you age it for six (6) months, then you should be able to get an equipment lease for about $40,000. The reason is that leasing companies will normally approve you for double the amount of your bank loan.

If you pay both of those on time and age them for another six (6) months, you can go back to the bank to request a credit line increase to $40,000. At the same time ask for a reduction on the interest you are being charged. The bank will look to see if you have "comparable credit" and they will see a $40,000 perfectly paid equipment lease. You may be approved and then you can age your credit line increase for another six (6) months and go back for another even larger equipment lease of say $80,000.

Gradually over a two year period and in intervals of six (6) months, you can build a very large credit line and the ability to be approved for very large equipment lease lines.

A similar principal can be applied to your business credit card available balances. Start out small and pay everything on time. Then after six (6) months, try to use the card to buy something over the credit limit. For example if your limit is $1,000, then try to buy something priced at $2,000. When ("if") you are turned down, ask to speak to the credit representative to request an increase in your available line. If you have paid on time and if you have built excellent business credit scores, you should get approved for the increase.

Because you have business credit cards with higher limits that have all been paid on time, and you have built excellent business credit card scores, your business mail box will begin to fill up with business credit card offers.

BE CAREFUL, just like with your personal credit, over doing it or trying to go too fast can destroy your business credit scores.

Don't Miss the Point of Building Business Credit

As we have consulted thousands of clients over the years, there is one consistent pattern that I continually see. Many of our clients misunderstand the importance of building their business credit. Too many want to build their business credit ONLY to get money, while one of the biggest benefits of building business credit is obtaining money that does not report to your personal credit file that is not the end result of our building business credit.

The main point is that you correctly build your business credit so that the financing you obtain is only the beginning. We are simply giving you the foundation and ground work to turn what amount of money you obtain in to a lot more as you continue the credit building process.

Rest assured whether you only obtain $40,000 or $200,000 if you continue the steps you will learn in our business credit building process you will be obtain to double, triple and many time quadruple the initial amount of money granted.

We hope that our Corporate Credit Program has served you very well and that you found the instruction and information vital to your business success.

www.corporatecreditconcepts.com

Bonus-

As a bonus, I have put together a special report on the **"8 Questions You Must Ask Before Working With Any Business Credit Building Company."** If you ask these questions you will know that you are working with a company with integrity and your credit building experience will be effective and efficient.

Please visit http://www.unlimitedbusinessfinancing.com to download this report.

You're on your way to excellent business credit scores!

Sincerely,

Chad and Trent Lee
Co-Founders

6130 Elton Ave
Las Vegas, NV 89107
702-216-0450

CPSIA information can be obtained
at www.ICGtesting.com
Printed in the USA
LVOW03s1300120617
537815LV00033B/1397/P

9 781934 275054